Screening and Discernment Instrument for Religious Life

A Workbook

Sr. Amy Hereford, csj
Attorney / Canonist
(c) 2018
www.ahereford.org

Published By Religious Life Project; Saint Louis, MO, USA, All rights reserved. http://religiouslifeproject.wordpress.com

All rights reserved. Without limiting the rights under copyright reserved above, no part of this publication may be reproduced, stored in or introduced into a retrieval system, or transmitted, in any form, or by any means (electronic, mechanical, photocopying, recording, or otherwise) without the prior written permission of the copyright owner of this book.

(c) Amy Hereford, 2018

email amyhereford@gmail.com for an electronic copy of this publication

Screening Instrument for Religious Life   (c) www.ahereford.org

Screening and Discernment Instrument for Religious Life

Table of Contents

For Vocation and Formation Directors:...7
Canon Law on Admission of Candidates..8
For Applicant:...9
Prayer for Vocations...9
How do I know if I am called?...10

Screening & Discernment Instrument for Religious Life..11
   A. Identifying Information...11
   B. Education..13
   C. Employment...15
   D. Activities..17
   E. Spiritual Life...19
   F. Vocational Discernment..23
   G. Family...27
   H. Personal & Behavioral..31
   I. Medical History...33
   J. Required Documents...35

Releases & Forms..36
   A. Psychological assessment – Release of Information:...36
   B. Letter of Reference - Form...36
   C. Medical Examination..38
   D. Dental Examination..40
   E. Ophthalmological Examination..41

Inventory of Legal and Financial Matters...43
   A. Religious and Marital Status..43
   B. Citizenship and Immigration Status...43
   C. Family and Fiduciary Responsibilities..44
   D. Health Care, Pension and Social Security...44
   E. Ministry, Business and Professional..45
   F. Banking and Financial Interests..46
   G. Real and Personal Property..47
   H. Debts and Liabilities...48
   I. Settlements and Other Legal and Professional Concerns...48

Name or initials: _____   Date Completed_____

Screening Instrument for Religious Life (c) www.ahereford.org 4

Name or initials: _____   Date Completed_____

Screening Instrument for Religious Life

Checklist	Given to Candidate (Date)	Returned (Date)	Follow-up
Application for Admission into Religious Life			
A. Identifying Information			
B. Education			
C. Employment			
D. Activities			
E. Spiritual Life			
F. Vocational Discernment			
G. Family			
H. Personal & Behavioral			
I. Medical Screening			
J. Required Documents			
Inventory of Legal and Financial Matters			
A. Citizenship and Immigration Status			
B. Religious and Marital Status			
C. Family and Fiduciary Responsibilities			
D. Health Care, Pension and Social Security			
E. Ministry, Business and Professional			
F. Banking and Financial Interests			
G. Real and Personal Property			
H. Debts and Liabilities			
I. Settlements and Other Legal and Professional Concerns			

Name or initials: _____   Date Completed_____

Screening Instrument for Religious Life

Name or initials: _____   Date Completed_____

For Vocation and Formation Directors:

This workbook is intended as a survey of a wide range of issues that arise in the screening and admission of candidates into a Religious Life. It covers areas that may arise with candidates who significant life experience. It is a screening instrument, intended to identify those areas of a candidate's background that will need more attention and discussion. It is not a substitute for good discernment, but an aid to it.

Each institute will supplement it with questions and conversations that are particular to its particular life, spirituality and mission, expanding the initial inquiry.

This is a workbook – it is not intended to be completed in one sitting. It can be used in a variety of ways.
- Give one or a few sections at a time to the applicant. When meeting with the applicant, take some time to go over those sections he/she has completed. Discuss any questions, comments, etc.
- Give the applicant the whole workbook – explaining that it is an instrument to guide discernment and explore issues that may arise as the process unfolds. Again, when meeting with the applicant, take some time to go over those sections that have been completed and discuss any questions, comments, etc.
- The Inventory of Legal and Financial Matters can be given to the candidate to fill in preliminary answers. This will identify any areas that may need further discussion. Preliminary answers can be discussed with the vocation director after which more documentation may be obtained if needed.

This workbook is help for those discerning a call to religious life with applicants. It does not replace the discernment process. Instead it is intended to help communities and inquirers to explore important areas that may need attention in the discernment process. The workbook is most valuable when it stimulates reflection by the candidate and subsequent discussion with the vocation director. The workbook may raise civil and canonical issues that may need further discussion in the vocation discernment process. Advice of an attorney and/or canonist familiar with vocation discernment may be helpful.

The brief introduction for Applicants on the next page may be given to them when you give or send parts of this workbook to them. The checklist on the previous page is intended to help you keep track of which sections have been given to the applicant, completed and reviewed within the community.

Blessings on your ministry,
Sr. Amy Hereford, CSJ, JD, JCD
amyhereford@gmail.com

Name or initials: _____   Date Completed_____

Canon Law on Admission of Candidates

CHAPTER III : THE ADMISSION OF CANDIDATES AND THE FORMATION OF MEMBERS

ARTICLE 1: ADMISSION TO THE NOVITIATE

Canon 641 The right to admit candidates to the novitiate belongs to the major Superiors, in accordance with the norms of the institute's own law.

Canon 642 Superiors are to exercise a vigilant care to admit only those who, besides being of required age, are healthy, have a suitable disposition, and have sufficient maturity to undertake the life which is proper to the institute. If necessary, the health, disposition and maturity are to be established by experts, without prejudice to can. 220.

Canon 643 §1 The following are invalidly admitted to the novitiate:
  1° One who has not yet completed the seventeenth year of age;
  2° a spouse, while the marriage lasts;
  3° one who is currently bound by a sacred bond to some institute of consecrated life, or is incorporated in some society of apostolic life, without prejudice to can. 684;
  4° one who enters the institute through force, fear or deceit, or whom the Superior accepts under the same influences;
  5° one who has concealed his or her incorporation in an institute of consecrated life or society of apostolic life.
 §2 An institute's own law can constitute other impediments even for the validity of admission, or attach other conditions.

Canon 644 Superiors are not to admit secular clerics to the novitiate without consulting their proper Ordinary; nor those who have debts which they are unable to meet.

Canon 645 §1 Before candidates are admitted to the novitiate they must produce proof of baptism and confirmation, and of their free status.
 §2 The admission of clerics or others who had been admitted to another institute of consecrated life, to a society of apostolic life, or to a seminary, requires in addition the testimony of, respectively, the local Ordinary, or the major Superior of the institute or society, or the rector of the seminary.
 §3 An institute's own law can demand further proofs concerning the suitability of candidates and their freedom from any impediment.
 §4 The Superiors can seek other information, even under secrecy, if this seems necessary to them.

Name or initials: _____   Date Completed_____

Screening Instrument for Religious Life   (c) www.ahereford.org

For Applicant:

All information in this Application will be held in confidence. Please type or write clearly. Be as honest and specific as possible in your answers.

This is not a test – it is a tool to help you explore your vocation and to assist the community in getting to know you and helping you explore your vocation and the potential 'fit' between you and our community. For this reason it is expected that it will take some time to work through the various partos of this booklet with your contact in the community.

Please reply to all questions and fill in all information. If the question does not apply to you, write "NO", "NONE" or "Does not apply". Please be complete in your answers. Some answers will require more space for an adequate response. Use the back of the paper and additional paper if necessary.

Prayer for Vocations

LORD of the Harvest,
BLESS young people with the gift of courage to respond to your call.
Open their hearts to great ideals, to great things.

INSPIRE all of your disciples to mutual love and giving—
for vocations blossom in the
good soil of faithful people.

INSTILL those in religious life, parish
ministries, and families with the confidence
and grace to invite others to embrace
the bold and noble path of a life
consecrated to you.

UNITE us to Jesus through prayer and sacrament,
so that we may cooperate
with you in building your reign of mercy
and truth, of justice and peace. Amen.

— Pope Francis (*Adapted from the Message on the 51st World Day of Prayer for Vocations*)

Name or initials: _____   Date Completed_____

How do I know if I am called?

People have asked on occasion: how do you know you are called? How do you know what you're called to? How do you know it is right for you? Really, how can anyone possibly know what God has in store for them?

It is an important question, but there is no easy answer. It is answered differently every time. How do I know? How did I know when I was in my twenties and I entered religious life? How do I know it is still right for me?

Religious life has three fundamental dimensions: **God, Community and Mission.**

Or, as we have come to say in my Sister of St. Joseph world, it's about **Community Spirituality Justice**

So first off, it's about God or Spirituality. Do I have a relationship with God? Is God tugging at my heart for a deeper relationship? Do I find joy and peace when I am with my God in prayer? as well as when I am living out of that God-relationship in community and in mission? God is the center of our lives, and in religious life, we live out of that centrality. We are privileged to have a lifetime of spiritual growth and development. And this is a gift that grounds the rest of our life, and enables us to share spirituality with all those we meet.

Second, it's about Community. Do I feel called to share my journey of spirituality and mission with other sisters or brothers who are committing to the same life journey? Do I have the skills to live in community? Can I share? trust? respect? love? Can I build community with all those God calls me to live with? Am I ready to do the work of community? - for a lifetime? There's no walking away when the times get tough, or someone gets on my nerves. We learn to love one another in our brokenness, and we love one another into wholeness. This wholeness does not mean that we never get on one another's nerves, it means that we have learned to reverence each other as gifts of God. We love and support each other in our differences, in our trials and in our joys.

Finally it's about Mission or Justice. We come together to see the world with God's eyes. To bring God's love in very concrete ways into our world. We do not bend the bruised reed or crush the smoldering wick. Instead we bring light into the dark places, hope to the despairing, joy to the sorrowful. We do this in concrete ways: by embracing the weak and the poor, by lifting up those that are bowed down, by bringing the healing, creative power of God to each person we meet and each place we inhabit.

Our lay brothers and sisters doing the same, in their particular vocation. In religious life, we do this in community, shaped by our spirituality and the vows. I thank God for this gift.

Name or initials: _____   Date Completed_____

Screening & Discernment Instrument for Religious Life

A. Identifying Information

Name (First and Last) _____

Address _____

City, State ZIP _____

Phone Number(s) _____

Email Address _____

Citizenship (and SSN) _____

Immigration Status _____

Date / Place of Birth _____

Current Age _____

Current Parish / Diocese _____

Name or initials: _____   Date Completed_____

Name or initials: _____   Date Completed_____

B. Education

Fill in the sections that are applicable.

	Date	Name	Place
Grade School(s):			

Graduation Date:

High School(s):

Graduation Date:

College(s), etc.:

Graduation Date:

Degree: Major: Minor:

Graduate School(s):

Graduation Date:

Degree: Field of Study: Minor:

Describe how you financed your education and any outstanding debt:

Name or initials: _____   Date Completed_____

Screening Instrument for Religious Life (c) www.ahereford.org 14

Name or initials: _____   Date Completed_____

C. Employment

List you employment beginning with present position and listing in reverse order. You may attach an up-to-date resume instead of filling in the following, but please provide reasons for leaving each position.

Date (Month & Year)	Name & Address of Employer	Position	Reason for Leaving
From: To:			
From: To:			
From: To:			
From: To:			
From: To:			
From: To:			
From: To:			

1. What is the greatest source of satisfaction in your work?

2. What is the least source of satisfaction in your work?

3. What brings you joy?

4. What do you find difficult? Frustrating? How do you handle it?

5. What are your gifts and talents?

6. How could your gifts and talents be put at the service of people in need?

(Use the back of the paper and additional paper if necessary.)

Name or initials: _____   Date Completed_____

Screening Instrument for Religious Life (c) www.ahereford.org 16

Name or initials:_____ Date Completed_____

Screening Instrument for Religious Life

D. Activities

List clubs, societies or social organizations of which you are or were member or held office.

	Name of Organization	Dates	Role
High School:			
College:			
Parish:			
Professional:			
Other:			

1. What volunteer or service activities are you or have you been engaged in? Please describe.

2. What type of reading do you prefer? Describe.

3. How do you spend your leisure time? What are your hobbies?

4. If you have had any significant travel experience, please describe. (Time, Place, Purpose)

(Use the back of the paper and additional paper if necessary.)

Name or initials: _____ Date Completed_____

Name or initials: _____   Date Completed_____

Screening Instrument for Religious Life　　　　　　　　　　(c) www.ahereford.org   19

E. Spiritual Life

What is the date and place of your:

	Date	Place
Baptism		
First Penance		
First Communion		
Confirmation		

Describe your formal instruction in the Catholic religion (if you did not attend Catholic schools). For example: CCD classes, convert classes, etc.

Are you a convert to Roman Catholicism? If "yes", when? Discuss.

Has there ever been a time you did not practiced Catholicism? Describe.

How do you keep informed about religious issues?

Indicate your participation in the following:

	Frequently	Occasionally	Seldom	Never
Celebration of Eucharist				
Sacramental Reconciliation				
Personal Prayer				
Christian Service				

Do you pray regularly? How often? When? Where? Describe.

Do you have a spiritual director? For how long?

(Use the back of the paper and additional paper if necessary.)

Name or initials: _____　　　　　　　Date Completed_____

Screening Instrument for Religious Life (c) www.ahereford.org 21

Have you discussed your vocation with your spiritual director? What insights have you gained?

If you do not have a spiritual director, is there any other person with whom you have discussed your vocation seriously? Over what period? What insights have you gained?

Has anyone tried to discourage you from following a religious vocation? If so, why?

Have you ever sought admission to another Congregation? If so, were you accepted? Please explain.

Have you ever been a member of another congregation? It so, give the following details: Name of Congregation, Address, Date of entrance, Date of leaving, Reasons for leaving. Any other pertinent information.

(Use the back and additional paper if necessary.)

Name or initials: _____   Date Completed_____

Screening Instrument for Religious Life (c) www.ahereford.org

Name or initials: _____   Date Completed_____

F. Vocational Discernment

How do you experience God's call in your life?

What do you know about religious life? What in this attracts you? What do you find challenging?

What are some of the things which you have not resolved and/or are unanswered questions?

Besides religious life, what other life work have you seriously considered for yourself?

When and how did you first encounter our community and/or its members?

Describe your relationship with our community.

(Use the back and additional paper if necessary.)

Name or initials: _____   Date Completed_____

Screening Instrument for Religious Life (c) www.ahereford.org 24

Name or initials: _____   Date Completed_____

Screening Instrument for Religious Life   (c) www.ahereford.org

What do you know about our community? What in this attracts you? What do you find challenging?

What particular elements of our spirituality do you identify with?

What particular elements of our community do you identify with?

What particular elements of our mission do you identify with?

How do you understand the difference between cloistered, contemplative life and active apostolic life? To which are you attracted and why?

(Use the back and additional paper if necessary.)

Name or initials: _____   Date Completed_____

Screening Instrument for Religious Life   (c) www.ahereford.org   26

Name or initials:_____   Date Completed_____

Screening Instrument for Religious Life   (c) www.ahereford.org   27

G. Family

Father's Name
Address
City, State ZIP
Age / Occupation
Deceased / Date
Religion / Practicing?

Mother's Name
Address
City, State ZIP
Age / Occupation
Deceased / Date
Religion / Practicing?

What is your father's attitude toward you: choice of a religious vocation?

What is your mothers attitude toward your choice of a religious vocation?

Are your parents married? Separated? Divorced? How long?

Is your father remarried? Date

Is your mother remarried? Date

With whom did you live when you were growing up?

(Use the back and additional paper if necessary.)

Name or initials: _____   Date Completed_____

Screening Instrument for Religious Life

List in order your brothers and sisters, starting with the oldest first and the youngest last (include your name in chronological order).

Name	Age	Grade/ Occupation	Deceased/ Date / Cause	Religion

Were there other members in your home while you were growing up?

Name / Relation	Age	Grade/ Occupation	Deceased: Date / Cause	Religion

As far as you can determine, is it likely that your parents or other members of your family will ever need your personal care or financial support? If so, please describe.

Briefly describe your father's personality as you would to a close friend who did not know him.

Briefly describe your mother's personality as you would to a close friend who did not know her

How do you feel about your parents' expectations of you?

Name or initials: _____   Date Completed_____

Screening Instrument for Religious Life   (c) www.ahereford.org

How frequently did your family move?

How would you describe family tension or conflict? __occasional __frequent __constant __seldom. Describe.

Describe where and with whom are you living now?

Have you had any dating experience? Describe

Have you ever been engaged? If yes, how long ago? For how long? What were your reasons for breaking the engagement?

Have you ever been married? Divorced? Had a marriage annulled?

Have you been sexually active? Been pregnant? Had any children?

Describe your sexual identity and orientation.

(Use the back and additional paper if necessary.)

Name or initials: _____   Date Completed_____

Name or initials: _____   Date Completed_____

H. Personal & Behavioral

Check which of the following would best describe you:

____ I have a group of friends with whom I do almost everything.
____ I have a few close friends and many acquaintances.
____ I have many acquaintances and no close friends.
____ I have one or two close friends.
____ I really don't think I have any friends; I'd like to have some friends.
____ I really don't think I have any friends; I don't feel I need any.

Most people have problems from time to time. What personal problems are you most aware of now? To whom do you go for help with your personal problems?

List in order of importance what you value most in life.

Would you like to improve yourself some way? If so, how?

Rate yourself in the following by placing an X in the appropriate column:

	5 High	4	3	2	1 Low
in self confidence					
in making hard decisions					
in courtesy					
in listening to people					
in willingness to accept criticism					
in being tactful with people					
in personal drive and ambition					
in religious practice					
in willingness to be taught					
in being tolerant of other's defects					
in living up to moral standards					
in ability to work under pressure					
in accuracy of work					
in ability to get along with others					
in assuming responsibility					

Name or initials: _____   Date Completed_____

in neatness of dress and personal grooming					
in handling anger					
in motivation for the religious life					
in expressing yourself					
in physical health					
in academic achievement					
in persuading others					
in capacity for silence					
in capacity for solitude					
in energy					
in sense of humor					
in ability to relax					
in overall personal maturity					

How do you think your friends would describe your personality?

What talents do you have?

How do you usually handle:

Success?

Tension?

Deadlines?

Compliments?

Failure?

Change?

Conflict?

How often do you use alcohol? ___daily ___weekly ___monthly ___less than monthly

Do you or have you used controlled substances (other than prescription drugs)?

Has drug or alcohol use ever been a problem? Have you received treatment? If yes, discuss.

Name or initials: _____   Date Completed_____

Screening Instrument for Religious Life

I. Medical History

1. Present Medical Conditions for which you are receiving treatment or medication. E.g. high blood pressure, allergies, injury, mood disorders.

2. Disabilities, allergies and dietary restrictions:

3. Past Medical History - major illnesses, injuries, hospitalizations or surgeries not mentioned above:

4. Psychological History – any diseases, major illnesses, addictions, hospitalizations or treatments not mentioned above:

5. Family History – list significant medical and psychological issues of your grandparents, parents, siblings, and children

6. Lifestyle Habits - diet, exercise, etc.

(Use the back and additional paper if necessary.)

Name or initials: _____   Date Completed_____

Screening Instrument for Religious Life (c) www.ahereford.org 34

Name or initials: _____   Date Completed_____

Screening Instrument for Religious Life

J. Required Documents

Submitted by Applicant:
 __Biographical data – Workbook part I, sections A-I
 __Autobiography in narrative form (5-10 pages)
 __Legal and Financial Inventory Workbook part II
 __Names and complete contact information of persons providing:
  Employment Reference (1)
  Personal References (3) e.g. pastoral minister, spiritual director, teacher, religious
  Reference from the leader of any previous religious communities you have been in
 __Signed releases of information for:
  References listed above
  Psychological and Behavioral Assessment
  Medical Information
 __Letter of request to be accepted for formation
 __Birth Certificate
 __Copy of Passport and Immigrant status if applicable
 __Baptismal Certificate
 __Marriage Certificate, divorce decree and decree of nullity (if applicable)
 __Transcripts from most recent educational institutions
 __Document on Remuneration (after acceptance, prior to arrival)

Submitted by others on behalf of applicant:
 __Physical exam (supplied by primary physician)
 __Vision exam (supplied by vision examiner)
 __Dental exam (supplied by dentist)
 __Psychological assessment
 __Behavioral assessment
 __Professional Licenses – statement of good standing
 __Criminal Check
 __Letter of affirmation by mentor
 __Letter of affirmation by Vocation Director
 __Letters from Personal References:
  How long have you known the person?
  In what capacity have you know the person?
  Describe the person generally?
  How would you assess the persons aptitude for religious life?

Name or initials: _____ Date Completed_____

Releases & Forms

A. Psychological assessment – Release of Information:

I understand that a psychological assessment is one of the requirements for admission to the [community], the Community.

I, the undersigned, agree to this psychological assessment. The nature and content of this assessment has been explained to me. I understand the parameters of confidentiality regarding the assessment and the report.

I agree to release the report, according to the release form I have signed for the psychologist, to the following person(s):

Leadership Designee: _____

Vocation Designee: _____

I also give permission for the above mentioned persons to be in consultation with the psychologist, after notifying me of this intent, if this is deemed advisable for my benefit or the benefit of the Community. I understand that the confidential nature of the report will be respected and that the information will only be used to assess my suitability for living vowed religious life in the Community.

I understand that the Psychologist will share with the Leadership Designee and Vocation Designee information deemed necessary to make an informed decision regarding my admission to the Community.

Applicant's Signature _____

Date _____

B. Letter of Reference - Form

In your letter of reference for [applicant] please describe:
1. How long have you known the applicant?
2. What is the nature of your association?
3. Are you aware of the applicant's interest in joining the [community]? Explain.
4. What would you describe as the applicant's greatest strengths and how are they exhibited?
5. What areas would you name as still needing growth for the applicant and why?
6. Any other comments you feel would be helpful?
7. What is your overall recommendation for this applicant to join [community]?
(Please Check One)
_____ An excellent applicant.
_____ A good applicant.
_____ An average applicant.
_____ A below average applicant
_____ I would not recommend the applicant.

Signed: _____ Phone: _____

Address: _____ E-mail: _____

Please return to [vocation director, community, address] in a sealed envelope.

Name or initials: _____ Date Completed_____

Screening Instrument for Religious Life

Assess specific qualities of applicant and give concrete examples of how the applicant lives the quality.

Characteristic	- Rating +	Comments
Getting along with others	1 2 3 4 5	
Making decisions	1 2 3 4 5	
Expressing feelings	1 2 3 4 5	
Working with others	1 2 3 4 5	
Working alone	1 2 3 4 5	
Accepting supervision	1 2 3 4 5	
Common sense	1 2 3 4 5	
Creativity	1 2 3 4 5	
Dependability	1 2 3 4 5	
Flexibility	1 2 3 4 5	
Living the faith	1 2 3 4 5	
Initiative	1 2 3 4 5	
Leadership ability	1 2 3 4 5	
Maturity	1 2 3 4 5	
Self confidence	1 2 3 4 5	
Sense of humor	1 2 3 4 5	
Sensitivity to others	1 2 3 4 5	
Sensitive to issues of Justice	1 2 3 4 5	
Accepting critical feedback	1 2 3 4 5	
Working under pressure	1 2 3 4 5	

Name or initials: _____   Date Completed_____

Screening Instrument for Religious Life   (c) www.ahereford.org 38

C. Medical Examination

To be completed by physician, physician assistant, or nurse practitioner at time of examination.

Name: _____ Date of Birth_____

Height _____Weight_____ Pulse_____ Respirations _____BP _____

General Appearance

_____

_____

_____

Please indicate normal or abnormal findings.

normal	abnormal		normal	abnormal	
		Nutrition			Thorax
		Skin			Breasts
		Head			Lungs
		Eyes			Heart
		Ears			Abdomen
		Nose			Hernia
		Sinuses			Pelvic exam
		Mouth			Rectal exam
		Thyroid			L. Spine
		C. Spine			Neurological exam
		Gastrointenstinal			Urinary
		Nodes			Extremities

Please comment on any of the above that are abnormal.

Name or initials: _____   Date Completed_____

Laboratory Data: (list abnormal findings)

Complete Blood Count_____

SMA-12_____ _____

Urinalysis_____

Pap smear_____

TB skin test/ chest x-ray_____

Mammogram_____

HIV_____

Summary:

Recommendations:

Signature of practitioner _____ *Date* _____

Printed Name: _____ Phone: _____

Address: _____ E-mail: _____

D. Dental Examination

This is to certify that _____ came to me for a dental examination on (date) _____.

Please comment on the results of your dental examination, listing any abnormalities you may have found.

_____ No treatment was necessary

_____ I have completed whatever treatment was necessary.

_____ I am in the process of treating her for _____

Signature of practitioner _____ *Date* _____

Printed Name: _____ Phone: _____

Address: _____ E-mail: _____

E. Ophthalmological Examination

This is to certify that _____ came to me for an ophthalmic examination on (date) _____.

Please comment on the results of your eye examination, listing any abnormalities you may have found.

_____ No treatment was necessary.

_____ I have completed whatever treatment was necessary.

_____ I am in the process of treating her for _____.

Signature of practitioner _____ **Date** _____

Printed Name: _____ Phone: _____

Address: _____ E-mail: _____

Inventory of Legal and Financial Matters

This inventory is intended to identify those areas that may require further attention or discussion as you continue your process of discernment of a vocation to religious life.

Instructions:
Mark X in the YES or NO column if no further inquiry is needed.
Mark O in the appropriate column if further inquiry or documentation is needed. Add an X when the documentation is obtained. Keep the documentation with this Checklist.

A. Religious and Marital Status

	YES	NO
1. Were you baptized Catholic? Please provide an official copy of baptismal certificate that is no more than 6 months old. (Six months requirement by Canon Law in order to determine if there exists any impediment, e. g., marriage, ordination, etc. which is to be entered on the reverse side of the baptismal certificate.)		
2. Are you confirmed? Please provide an official copy of the confirmation certificate.		
3. Have you ever been married? If YES, at the time of marriage what religion was being practiced?		
If YES, was marriage in the Roman Catholic Church? If NO, please explain.		
4. Widowed or divorced?		
If divorced, has a decree of nullity been issued? YES NO (obtain a copy)		
5. Are there any living children? If YES, list names and ages.		
Is there any responsibility for any of the children? If YES, please explain.		

B. Citizenship and Immigration Status

	YES	NO
1. Are you a citizen of the US? If naturalized provide documentation. If NO, country of birth? Citizenship? Provide documentation of Immigration status.		

C. Family and Fiduciary Responsibilities

	YES	NO
1. Do you have any responsibility for any other family member? If YES, please explain.		
2. Are you responsible for the personal or financial care of another? If YES, describe the scope of responsibility		
3. Are you court-appointed legal guardian of another person? If YES, provide the name, age and place of residence of the ward, relationship to the individual in addition to this guardianship.		
4. Representative Payee for someone on Medicare or Medicaid? If YES, please explain the name, age and place of residence of this person, and the reason why serving.		
5. Power of Attorney for business matters for any individual(s)? If YES, please explain the name, age and place of residence of this person, and the reason why serving.		
6. Designated as Durable Power of Attorney for Health Care for any individual(s)? If YES, please explain the name, age and place of residence of this person, and the reason why you are designated.		
7. Administrator or Executor of another's will? If Yes, in what state will the estate be probated? Please explain details.		
8. Administrator or Executor of any estate? If Yes, has the estate been probated and all matters settled?		
If NO, what is the timeliness for final settlement? In what state is this action?		

D. Health Care, Pension and Social Security

	YES	NO
1. Do you have health care coverage? If YES, how long will that coverage be available? What is the monthly premium? Who is responsible for paying the premium?		
2. Do you have a signed Durable Power of Attorney for Health Care? If YES, who is named? (Please provide a copy.)		
3. Do you have a Living Will? (Please provide a copy.)		
4. Have you received a Social Security earnings statement and reviewed it for accuracy? (Please provide a copy.)		
5. Have you worked the required quarters to be eligible for Social Security benefits? If NO, now many quarters of coverage?		

6. Are you currently receiving a Social Security benefit? Amount?		
7. Are you currently receiving another retirement or disability benefit? Amount?		
8. Are you entitled to pension at retirement? Source(s)? Amount(s)?		
9 Do you have any individual retirement accounts (e.g., IRAS, Roth IRAS, SEPS, 401K, 403B, etc.) or other deferred accounts in your name? If YES, what are the types, location, and terms? (Please provide documentation.)		

E. Ministry, Business and Professional

	YES	NO
1. Are you currently employed or in ministry?		
If YES, is there a contract? If YES, what are the terms		
2. Are you qualified or licensed in stated profession? If YES, please provide documentation. If NO. determine what is needed.		
3. Does your profession require re-certification? If Yes, what is needed?		
4. Does profession require professional insurance? If YES, who pays the premium and what is the amount?		
5. Do you own a business in whole or in part? If YES, please provide details, and type of ownership.		
Are there any outstanding liabilities related to the business? If YES, please explain.		
Ever filed for bankruptcy for the business? If YES, please explain.		
6. Do you currently serve as a member on a Board of Directors/Trustees? If YES, please explain.		
7. Do you bear any financial responsibility for this? If YES, please explain.		
8. Is your Board service covered by appropriate insurance?		

F. Banking and Financial Interests

	YES	NO
1. Do you have an account in any financial institution (checking, savings, money market, credit union, etc.) in own name? (Obtain statement)		
2. Are you named on an account in any financial institution with another person? If YES, please explain.		
3. Is your Social Security Number used on any account other than those named above? If YES, please explain.		
4. Do you any investments in own name? If YES, what are the types, location, and terms?		
5. Do you receive any income from any investments not listed solely in your name? If YES, please explain.		
6. Do you receive dividend income from any stocks, bonds, annuities, etc? If YES, please provide a complete description where the dividends are deposited and approximately how much received yearly.		
7. Do you have any investments not listed solely in you name? If YES, please provide a complete description.		
8. Do you have an administrator for your finances? If YES, please provide a copy of the administration instrument, name of the administrator and where finances are located.		
9. Do you have any mineral rights on which royalties are received in you name? If YES, please provide the source, terms, amounts, etc.		
10. Do you receive income from royalties or other contractual arrangements? If YES, please provide the source, terms, amounts, etc.		
11. Are there any other areas in which you may have a financial interest or from which income is received that has not been asked above? If YES, please provide a complete description:		
12. Have you ever filed for personal bankruptcy? If YES, what is the status of that filing? Please explain.		
13. Do you have a life insurance policy? If YES, what is the monthly premium? for how long? Who is the beneficiary?		
14. Are you the beneficiary under any life insurance policies? If YES, please provide the name of the insurance company and under whose policy individual is the beneficiary.		
15. Do you have any profit sharing plans? If YES, please provide the name of the plan, the plan number and the terms.		

16. Do you have or anticipate receiving in the near future any stocks, bonds, or any other property received either by will or outright gifts for which individual has made no provisions? If YES, please provide a complete description of the situation, including reasons why no provisions have yet been made for same.		
17. Is there a trust in your name? If YES, please provide a complete description. Who is the Trustee?		
18. Are you the Beneficiary under a trust? If Yes, what are the conditions under which you may or may not draw benefits? Who is the Trustee?		
19. Do you currently receive income from a trust? If YES, in what amounts? How often?		
20. Are you named a trustee under a trust? If YES, please provide a copy of the trust.		

G. Real and Personal Property

	YES	NO
1. Do you own or have an interest in a home, condominium, time-share or any other such dwelling?		
If YES, do you own with clear title? If NO, please explain.		
Are the property and contents adequately insured?		
Is property subject to a mortgage? If YES, how much per month?		
2. Do you own any real estate other than what is named in #1 above? If YES, please describe. Describe how is the land being utilized?		
3. Are you leasing or renting property by yourself or with another? If YES, please explain.		
4. Do you own an automobile/vehicle in your name?		
5. If YES, do you have insurance which meets state requirements? If YES, please provide the name of the insurance agency, type of insurance, who is covered, amount of coverage and the amount of and who pays the premium. If NO, please provide an explanation.		
6. Are you using a car that is not your own? (E.g. family, friend, leased) If YES, please explain.		
7. Have you ever created any materials (books, music, computer programs, etc) on which you continue to receive royalties? If YES, what amounts and for how long will these royalties be received?		
8. Do you have personal property wish to retain (Furniture, electronic equipment,		

	YES	NO
music, etc)? Describe.		
9. Do you have personal property wish to use in the community (Furniture, electronic equipment, music, etc)? Describe.		
10. Do you have a valid will?		

H. Debts and Liabilities

	YES	NO
1. Do you have any credit cards? If YES, please provide a list of the name(s) of the credit cards, the amounts due.		
2. Do you have any credit card debts (more than 60 days overdue)? If YES, please provide payment plan.		
3. Are you repaying a college loan? If YES, what is the outstanding balance? Monthly payments? Explain any special terms or deferments.		
4. Do you have any other outstanding loans? If YES, please provide a list of all identifying the holder of the note, terms of payment, outstanding balance.		
5. Do you have current and future tax (federal, state, local) liabilities? If YES, please explain.		
6. Are there any other liabilities and/or anything owed to another not mentioned elsewhere? If YES, please explain.		

I. Settlements and Other Legal and Professional Concerns

	YES	NO
1. Are you currently receiving any money from the settlement of a lawsuit or insurance claim? If YES, please provide the terms of the settlement.		
2. Are you currently receiving any money from the settlement of a worker's compensation action? If, YES, what are the terms of the settlement?		
3. Are you a party in any litigation concerning previous professional or personal misconduct? If YES, please provide a complete description:		
4. Have you ever been convicted of a felony or violent crime? If YES, please provide full details:		
5. Do you individual currently retain the professional services of an attorney? If YES, how are fees handled?		
6. Do you individual currently retain the professional services of a financial		

manager? If YES, how are fees handled?		
7. Do you individual currently retain the professional services of another financial or legal professional? If YES, how are fees handled?		

Made in the USA
Monee, IL
14 September 2020